On The Beach

CHANCE PORTRAITS FROM TWO SHORES

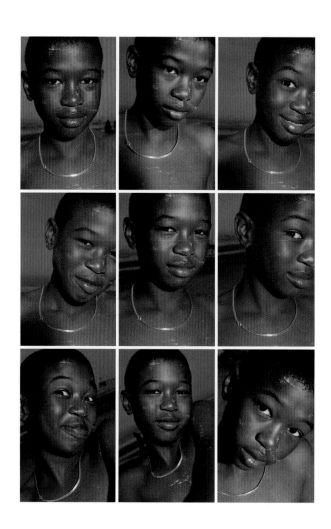

On The Beach
CHANCE PORTRAITS FROM TWO SHORES

Douglas McCulloh • Jacques Garnier

Forward by Kevin Miller
Essay by Tyler Stallings

SOUTHEAST MUSEUM OF PHOTOGRAPHY

On the Beach: Chance Portraits on Two Shores

Published by the Southeast Museum of Photography,
Daytona Beach Community College, Florida

Photographs and Essays © 2006 by Douglas McCulloh and Jacques Garnier

"Forward" © 2006 by Kevin Miller

"Empathy Is in the Details: On the Portraiture in Jacques Garnier and Douglas McCulloh's *On the Beach*" © 2006 by Tyler Stallings

On the Beach: Chance Portraits on Two Shores
McCulloh, Douglas; Garnier, Jacques.

ISBN 978-0-9789072-0-4
Library of Congress Control Number: 2006933222
    1. Photography, Artistic.
    2. McCulloh, Douglas, 1956–, Garnier, Jacques, 1948–.
    3. Title

Cover and book design, book production: Discharge/New York
Custom exhibition prints—California photographs: Iris Lee, New York
Custom exhibition prints—Florida photographs: Douglas McCulloh and Jacques Garnier
Scans and digital color management: Photomation, Anaheim, California
Prepress: Bright Arts, Hong Kong
Printing and binding: Imago, Singapore

Orders, inquiries, and correspondence should be addressed to:
        Southeast Museum of Photography
        Daytona Beach Community College
        1200 W. International Speedway Blvd.
        P.O. Box 2811
        Daytona Beach, FL 32120-2811
        www.smponline.org

Dedicated to the memory of
Kevin Jon Boyle—artist, curator, and surfer—who made an art of life
and lived a long while at the ocean's edge.

Special thanks to the following:

Kevin Miller, Director, Southeast Museum of Photography
for enabling the Florida portion of the photography and directly facilitating this book.

Jonathan Green, Director, UCR/California Museum of Photography
for comments, ideas, and assistance in arranging California photography locations.

Tyler Stallings, Chief Curator, Laguna Art Museum
for support, comment, and counsel.

Tim B. Wride, Curator of Photography, Los Angeles County Museum of Art
for interest, advice, and assistance in arranging California photography locations.

Forward

By 2004 Douglas McCulloh and Jacques Garnier had already been working on an extensive series of images of people at Southern California beaches for four years and had drawn together a compelling and fascinating array of photographs. When they approached the Southeast Museum of Photography with this work, we immediately saw potential parallels and connections that could be created if they extended the series. We thought that they could develop some new chapters with photographs made on Florida beaches.

Both Douglas and Jacques were keen to elaborate on their project in Florida and immediately saw some of the contrasts, affinities and tensions that two distinct series of subjects would inevitably bring to the project. It was clear that the divergent cultures, the markedly different sense of place, and even the likely demographic differences between the subjects in these two locales would yield a rich and rewarding series. In 2005 they set about working in Florida. Over the intervening year-and-a-half Douglas and Jacques have worked with boundless enthusiasm, verve and energy to bring this wonderful project to its present shape.

This book accompanies an exhibition of the same name at The Southeast Museum of Photography. Both forms of this wonderful project are a testament to the passion, imagination and commitment that are the hallmarks of how Douglas and Jacques approach their art. Photography, in some hands, is a tool capable of carving out of the lumpen reality around us a refined, coherent and intelligible vision of order and meaning. *On the Beach* achieves this with a rich and complex allusiveness that is deeply informed by the traditions of the medium.

Kevin Miller is director of the Southeast Museum of Photography, Daytona Beach, Florida.

Introduction

by Douglas McCulloh and Jacques Garnier

I. On Chance Operations

On the Beach rises from a powerfully straightforward idea—go to beaches and capture a chance sample of beachgoers. The idea of sampling drives the project. In the words of artist Sol LeWitt, "the idea becomes a machine that makes the art."

Our strategy is direct and guileless. We take up a fixed location on the sand and post a sign inviting all who pass to have their photograph taken. We sample the passing parade like scientists who periodically dip water out of a flowing stream.

The ocean's edge is a place of freedom and desire, a place to stare and to strut, to see and to be seen. Beaches are half display, half voyeurism. This is the precise terrain of photography—one side posing, the other looking. Cameras belong on the beach.

We bring a single camera and lens. To keep lighting consistent, we bring the inside out. We plant a studio lighting setup directly in the sand. At times the rising tide has swirled around the base of our light stands. We use the beach and ocean as our backdrop. Our crisp strobe lights echo and reinforce the hard light of the sun.

On the Beach is built on a foundation of chance. For the Surrealists, chance is the purest method of encountering what André Breton calls marvelous beauty. He writes that the perception of this marvelous beauty is akin to fear or sexual desire—a primal experience beyond the intellectual realm. Breton holds that beauty cannot be deliberately created. It can only be released or discovered, and a central way to achieve this is to accept the offerings of chance.

Composer John Cage, too, adopts the world's very mode of operation—contingency and chance—as the method best-suited to fully embrace its complexity and irrationality. Cage uses non-intention and chance operations "to introduce an audience, not to the specialized world of art, but to the open, unpredictable open world of everyday living." We use our chance encounters with beachgoers, our random sample from the passing crowd, to cut through the mythologies of beach culture and engage the marvelous actual. The goal, Cage says, should be to present "things as they come, as they happen, rather than as they are possessed or kept or forced to be."

We have a ritual: we arrive with the early morning light. We plant the splayed legs of our light stands in the sand and adjust the camera settings. Our equipment is simple and our approach simpler. We put traditional beach photography tactics off limits. We do not shoot idealized beach denizens with long lenses like journalists, surf mag photogs, or voyeurs. We do not capture detailed beach vistas with massive view cameras. We do not roam the beach with wide angle lenses like sunstruck Winograds. We do not shoot in the waves or from the pier. In fact, we don't move at all. We stay in one place and simply sample the passing parade. We stand with toes in the sand, camera at hand, awaiting the poetry of chance.

Edward Weston writes: "I take advantage of chance—which in reality is not chance—but being ready, attuned to one's surroundings—and grasp my opportunity in a way which no other medium can equal in spontaneity, while the impulse is fresh, the excitement strong. The nearest to photography is a quick line sketch, done usually as a note for further elaboration. And how much finer, stronger, more vivid these sketches usually are than the finished painting."

A surprising majority of passersby consent to stand before our strobe lights. They bring their friends and family. Sometimes there are lines. Both of us shoot. We hand the single camera back and forth. We are not certain which of us made many of the photographs.

As we photograph the flow of subjects, we emulate the surfer. The surfer is small and the ocean forceful. Each interaction between wave and surfer is beyond prediction, unique and uncontrollable. Shifting change is the only constant of the sea. There can be no victory. In fact, the metaphor of contest itself is an illusion. Grace in surfing must be based on creative flexibility and perceptive accommodation. Like the surfer, we attempt to engage the shifting circumstance of the world before our lens with perception, flexibility, responsiveness, and balance.

We capture the particular—a growing series of individuals, an omnivorous, indifferent, and democratic sample. "There is no other art with as great a democratic capacity as photography," says photographer Manuel Alvarez Bravo. When you accumulate enough chance particulars, you build a portrait of the whole. Hamzah Fansuri, a contemporary of Shakespeare and the most esteemed poet of the Indonesian archipelago, writes: "The sea is eternal: when it heaves/ One speaks of the waves but in reality they are the sea." (jlg & dfm)

II. Art and the Portrait

By last count there are over six-and-a-half billion faces, all of them unique. We gaze at them, we analyze them, we laugh at them, we cry with them and feel for them. We see their strengths and their vulnerabilities as reflections of our own. So it's no surprise that the face has captivated audiences since the early Greeks who demanded that their likenesses be as perfect as possible, to the point of creating an "ideal." By the time of Alexander in the 4th century B.C., the rendering of an ideal was astonishing, almost too perfect. The Romans felt a need to be more representative, making portraits that were less perfect but more realistic. By the time of the Renaissance, artists were paid by the wealthy to create portraits celebrating power and defying mortality, often creating masterpieces of flattery. Leonardo's Mona Lisa defies categorization through the enigma of her smile and the movement of her gaze. Goya, on the other hand, in the early 19th century showed no pity to his subjects and imbued the features of his sitters with all their vanity and ugliness, their greed and emptiness.

Photography triggered an important change in the evolution of portraiture. The portrait, which to this point had been available only to the well-to-do, was now available to all—the camera becoming a great equalizer. In the mid-nineteenth century, portrait studios swiftly cropped up in major cities all over the world. Now a sitter would stand or sit still, perched in front of a backdrop for seconds or even minutes as the slow photo emulsion soaked up light. Stiff and often wooden-like, these photographs were planned encounters.

"Portraits are often about the way that the real space is organized," writes photography critic A. D. Coleman. "This unlocks the secrets, this tells the story, this confides to the surface the information that is to unfold. It becomes impossible to separate the space from the intent. As in physics: 'observation changes the nature of the situation observed.'"

The portraits of *On The Beach* are fast, aggressive, and chaotic. Through rigorous framing, energetic cropping and spontaneous interaction, an almost surrealistic dialogue commences. There is no preconceived notion to order or elicit certain expressions. As Flaubert continued his search for "le mot juste" and Henri Cartier-Bresson his "decisive moment," the ideal moment with these beach portraits arises from a spontaneous ballet between the models who are free to do as they wish and the photographer who is looking for a moment of magic. Not every encounter is free or magical. And yet, there is a great effort to be "truthful" which is certainly not the same as being "the truth." The dialogue between the cameraperson and the subject is delicate and precarious, often reinventing itself from moment to moment.

While many portraits are static, often posed with a backdrop, we use nature—the beach—as the backdrop. Our effort is to make the process more of a dialogue, an interactive act of creation where the subject creates the mood and the photographer picks the moment. Diane Arbus writes: "I remember a long time ago when I first began to photograph I thought, there are an awful lot of people in the world and it's going to be terribly hard to photograph all of them, so if I photograph some kind of generalized human being, everybody'll recognize it. It'll be like what they used to call the common man or something. It was my teacher, Lisette Model, who finally made it clear to me that the more specific you are, the more general it'll be."

By sampling, by shooting thousands of beach portraits, an almost scientific sampling edges closer and closer to the concept of "*the* beachgoer." Who is this elusive "beachgoer?" Someone who sports different attire, if any, who is not afraid to disrobe and show flesh to strangers, who communes and plays with a nature that is so interwoven with summertime that the other seasons seem not to exist. Smiles, sunburns, silliness and playfulness seem to coexist with the sights and sounds of the surf. Our purpose is to interact without intruding, to capture a moment without planning, to be truthful without artifice, and to pay tribute to life *On The Beach*.

(jlg)

III. Shooting On the Beach

Photographing people on beaches is an aggression.

The beach eliminates conceits, concealment, and clothing. It removes everyday roles, stances, and status. The beach is a set of subtractions. When you cross onto the sand you become a little naked.

To the equation of vulnerability, we add unforgiving studio lights and a ruthless high-resolution camera. Then we wait to see what happens before the lens. In truth, we are setting a trap.

The beach itself aids our trickery. People believe the beach is a place of relaxation, of diversion, of unbuttoned behavior. And belief is transformative. Beachgoers bring these ideas with them when the cross from city to strand. This doctrine of the incautious beach becomes a license for the unfeigned, the spontaneous. Beachgoers are remarkably unguarded. They remain so even when standing in front of our 2000 watt-second strobe lights with eighteen-inch, hard-white reflectors. Everyone's guard is down at the beach. Photographers love unguarded moments; they're best for ambush.

Photographer Diane Arbus said: "The camera is cruel, so I try to be as good as I can to make things even." That's a lovely sentiment, but goodness is not our agenda. Instead, our central pursuit is what writer James Agee called "the effort to perceive simply the cruel radiance of what is." The task takes an unblinking eye and a hard heart. When someone comes along and stands before our camera—as have hundreds—we trip our shutter. If this straightforward tactic is sometimes cruel, so be it.

We don't goad or incite our subjects; we don't need to. We greet people and identify the area of light in front of our strobes. We let people situate themselves. We tell them, "Do whatever you like," and they do. If the resulting image occasionally seems like a sucker punch, it's entirely self-inflicted; our subjects deal themselves the blow. We have only a few rules, (and they're just for us): pay attention, never look away, don't censor, and let the shutter snap like the permanent snare that it is. In Susan Sontag's memorable phrase, each photograph is a "soft murder."

Photographs, even murderous ones, only capture exteriors, skin, veneer. I don't believe portraits go below the surface. "They don't go below anything," wrote Richard Avedon, "they're readings of what's on the surface. I have great faith in surfaces. A good one is full of clues." These are photographs full of hints and intimations, suggestions and suspicions.

Photographer Walker Evans was a trenchant observer and pitiless writer. "[Photography] is not cute cats," he wrote, "nor nudes, motherhood, or arrangements of manufactured products. Under no circumstances is it anything ever anywhere near a beach." Here is our best defense against Evans' comment: these images are not about the beach. These are portraits of unguarded people captured at a place of transformation. In any event, our task is to make the photos as they come along. Your job is to decide what they mean.

On a bright autumn day when I was young, I went swimming in the Mediterranean near Naples. I entered from a rocky beach that I regarded as hopelessly skimpy by California standards and waded into unruffled, indifferent water. I floated on my back and looked up at the cerulean sky, same as it ever was. I sculled slowly away out into the Tyrrhenian Sea toward Capri. Mount Vesuvius came into view to the east, unstable and draped with wisps of sulphur. I stopped. How deep was the water? Twelve feet? I didn't know at the time and definitely cannot be certain now.

I hung in the luminous water and looked down. Below me—shining aquamarine and sunspotted blue—I thought I saw the corner of a structure. Angular, vague, eroded, but comprehensible. A platform? A foundation? The base of a fallen arch? It was unmistakably manmade. I paddled slowly and stared down. I puzzled out a pair of toppled columns, bent like crooked arms. Then a curve of stones and a scatter of rectangles, tipped and tangled in the wreckage.

"In Rome, seaside pursuits were the lifeblood of civilized pleasures," write Lena Lencek and Gideon Bosker in their social history of the beach. From the end of the republic to the height of the empire, ostentatious beachside villas filled the shore from Ostia to Naples.

On Capri—behind me in the Bay of Naples—Emperor Tiberius built himself twelve luxuriant villas, naming each after a god. At his beachside retreat at Centum Cellae, Emperor Trajan used slaves from the corners of the empire to excavate a bathing and boating harbor, complete with a sheltering pleasure island. At Alisium, Pompey the Great built a sumptuous retirement home with marble walls, rich mosaics, lead plumbing and luminescent isinglass panels. Eventually, competition for coastal vistas became so fevered that Emperor Justinian the Great enacted a strict ordinance protecting existing ocean views by controlling seaside construction. Meanwhile, the finest writers of Rome penned chronicles of pleasures by the shore—Cicero, Seneca, Statius, Pliny the Younger. "How mighty is the beauty of the sea," wrote Cicero, "the view of its immensity, the manifold isles, and delightful coasts."

I drifted in the azure sea, the Isola di Capri behind me, Mount Vesuvius before me. I hung in the cool water above the flooded city—floating above villas, terraces, and temples wrecked by history and submerged by the shifting shoreline.

If you read the beach as a text, one metaphor is central—erasure. Let us reiterate the obvious. Your passage may leave traces in the sand, but the waves will erase them beyond all recovery. Children may sculpt sand castles and raise defensive walls, but the overnight tide will leave the slate blank, always, forever. The Assyrians, Phoenicians, Greeks, Romans, and we, too, may build our cities along the shore, but the beach is a mutable place stranded between sea and land, not quite either one. The word "shore" itself is anchored in an etymology of change. Shore derives from the Old English *scieran*: "to cut, to shear;" land and lives can be suddenly shorn away along the shore. Today, we again live in a rich culture that, like the Romans, prizes the ocean's edge. The cycles of change that literally engulfed Rome are inexorable. "History doesn't repeat itself," wrote Mark Twain, "but it does rhyme."

Erasure, of course, merely sets the stage for a rewrite. The beach has long been seen as a place of reinvention, of transformation. "In classical myth," write Lencek and Bosker, "the shoreline is typically a place where identity itself is imperiled and the self becomes unrecognizable—changed according to the whimsy of the gods." At the beach, writes Anne Morrow Lindbergh in her memoir *Gift from the Sea*, "one becomes, in fact, like the element on which one lies, flattened by the sea; bare, open, empty as the beach, erased by today's tides of all yesterday's scribbling."

The beach, more than any other place on the planet, reveals the cycles of change. Erasure, transformation, and renewal wash over the everyday like waves over the sand. Some cycles are at human scale: the sun rises and sets, the tide floods and ebbs, photographers come and go. Other cycles are exceedingly long: shorelines shift, civilizations are swallowed by time and water, great oceans form only to evaporate. Beneath the snow at the summit of Mount Everest are marine fossils.

The technology of photography is remarkably suited to serve the human desire to make this moment, this precise moment, endure. It's a spiritual sentiment. Photography on the beach—a place of extreme flux where the effects of time are mercilessly apparent—carries a special poignancy. Allen Ginsberg, famed as a poet, but also a persistent photographer, wrote: "The sacramental quality [of photographs] comes from an awareness of the transitory nature of the world, an awareness that it's a mortal world, where our brief time together is limited and it's the one and only occasion when we'll be together."

(*dfm*)

Empathy Is in the Details: On the Portraiture in Jacques Garnier and Douglas McCulloh's *On The Beach*

by Tyler Stallings

Jacques Garnier and Douglas McCulloh's project *On the Beach*, is also the title for Nevil Shute's 1957 novel. Shute's story is a post-apocalyptic tale set in Australia, mostly Melbourne, which has become a last refuge after World War III. However, deadly clouds of radioactive fallout are drifting southward. The Aussies resign themselves to their fate and the novel describes their attempts at daily rituals that focus on the details of life in order to keep their minds from contemplating the incomprehensible form of approaching death. For them, the devil is not in the details, but in the inconceivable, which is death, where the imagination may run rampant forming fantasies full of havoc.

Both Shute's *On the Beach* and Garnier/McCulloh's *On the Beach* depict the beach as a setting that blends the details of life and the unimaginable, that is, reality and fantasy, of the land that butts up against it and of the ocean that stretches outward, of the past in the rear and of the future in the front. Garnier and McCulloh's artistic sensibilities bring to mind those in the photographic portraits by Rineke Dijkstra (b.1959), Richard Avedon (1923-2004), Diane Arbus (1923–1971), and August Sander (1876–1964). They all created portraits with a formal and restrained composition. Sometimes, their subjects were isolated within their environments or even abstracted from them. Dijkstra's adolescents on the beach were evenly split in the middle by the beach and the ocean, with no other accompanying details. Avedon posed his cowboys, miners, and drifters for his *In the American West* series with a portable backdrop of white studio paper. This imposed uniformity towards their subjects objectifies them, though not in a dehumanizing manner. Rather, a kind of extreme empathy appears because the sameness of the background allows the viewer to focus on the subject's individual details.

In a sense, they are like Shute's characters, who go about their daily rituals in order to avoid contemplating an uncontrollable approach of death, but under their surfaces the dread and fear can be seen when unguarded moments are caught on film.

In this respect, Garnier and McCulloh run counter to the commercial work of surf photography which is geared to aggrandize and elevate competitive surfers and their corporate sponsors. There is a very interesting and yet untapped (by the art world) body of work by surf photographers like Art Brewer, Anthony Friedkin, and Craig Steyck, which bears further thought and comparison to Garnier and McCulloh's project. Artworld entrenched artists like Catherine Opie (b. 1961) recently have touched upon surfing as subject, but to no great depth unfortunately.

Garnier and McCulloh's odd beach populace are more akin to those found in Diane Arbus' New York City or August Sander's Germany who, each in their own ways, approached their native lands as unfamiliar ones. Arbus looked to the margins of society with children, carnival performers, transvestites, and eccentrics of all sorts. Sander envisioned his *People of the Twentieth Century* as a far-reaching visual record of the German masses, grouping them into categories, ranging from Farmer to Woman to Artists to the City, and even one called Last People, comprised of the elderly and the deformed.

In the cases of all these artists, their portraits are not only documentaries, but allegories for their times—Sander working during Nazi Germany; Arbus in postwar America; Avedon in Reagan's America; and Dijkstra's present-day adolescents. Similarly, Garnier and McCulloh do not attempt to improve on the reality in front of their lens (suggestive of a kind of return to straight photography in a digital imaging age). All of their subjects face the camera, knowing that they are collaborating in the process of making their own portraits.

Garnier and McCulloh, and their colleagues of portraiture in the past and the present, are exploring the self-conscious relationship between how we portray ourselves and how others project upon on us, and the subtle line between fantasy and faith. Lastly, they explore the more specific setting of the beach as a site where people are in a state of transition. *On the Beach* the acting out, the acts of joy, the seeming classlessness, defy for a moment the existential awareness of our inherent isolation as human beings.

Tyler Stallings is the chief curator at Laguna Art Museum, Laguna Beach, California. He was a co-curator for the museum's ground-breaking exhibition, *Surf Culture—The Art of Surfing*, which toured the U.S. and Australia from 2002 to 2003.

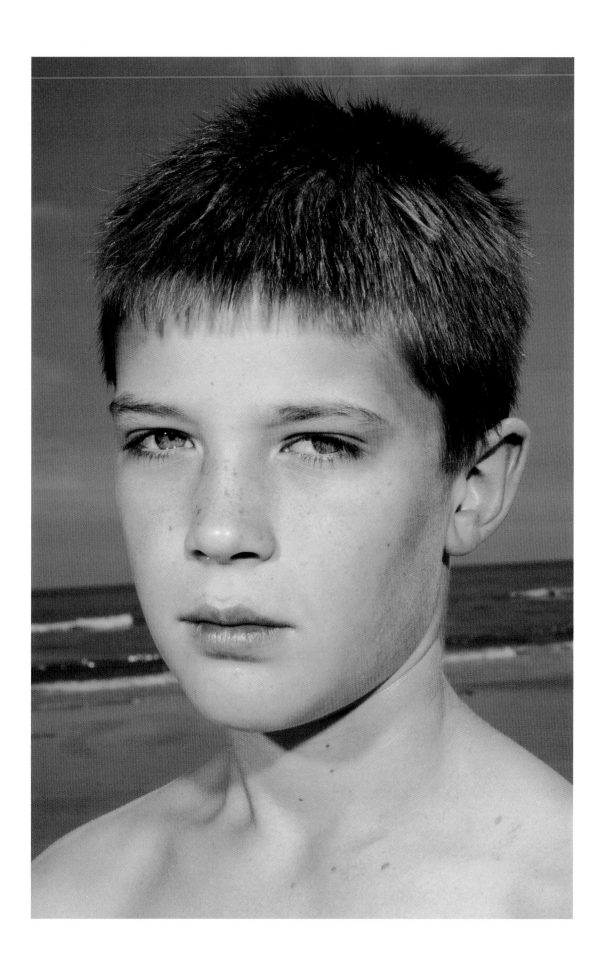

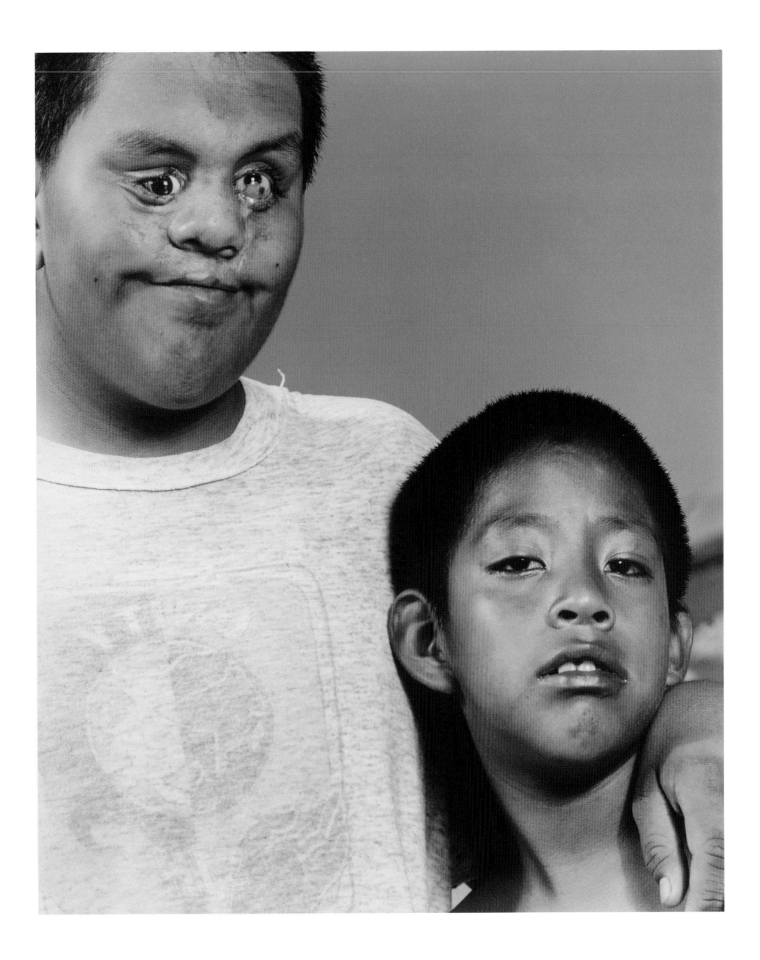

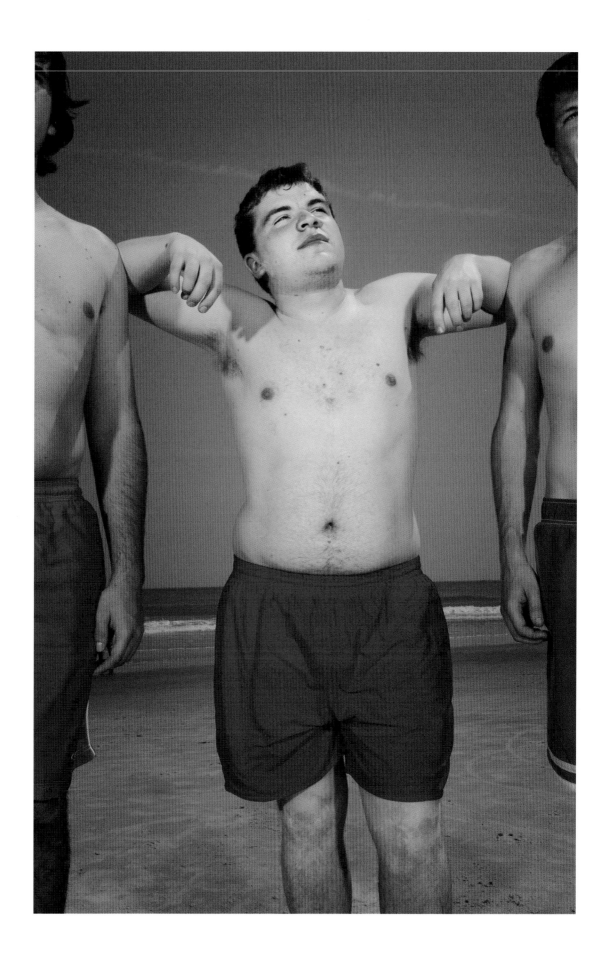

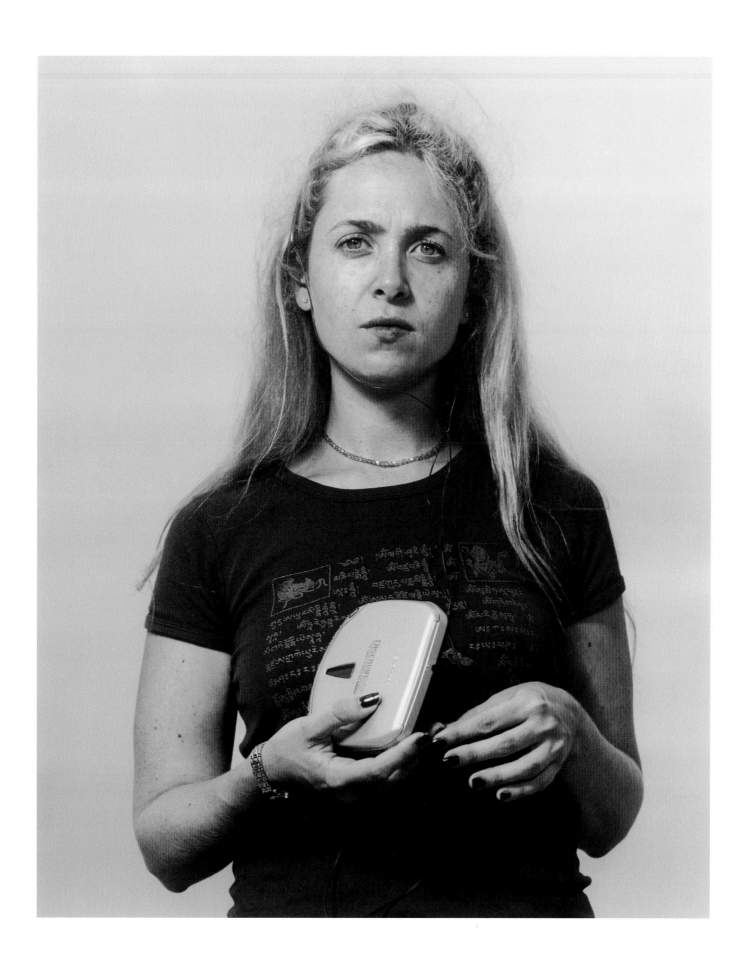

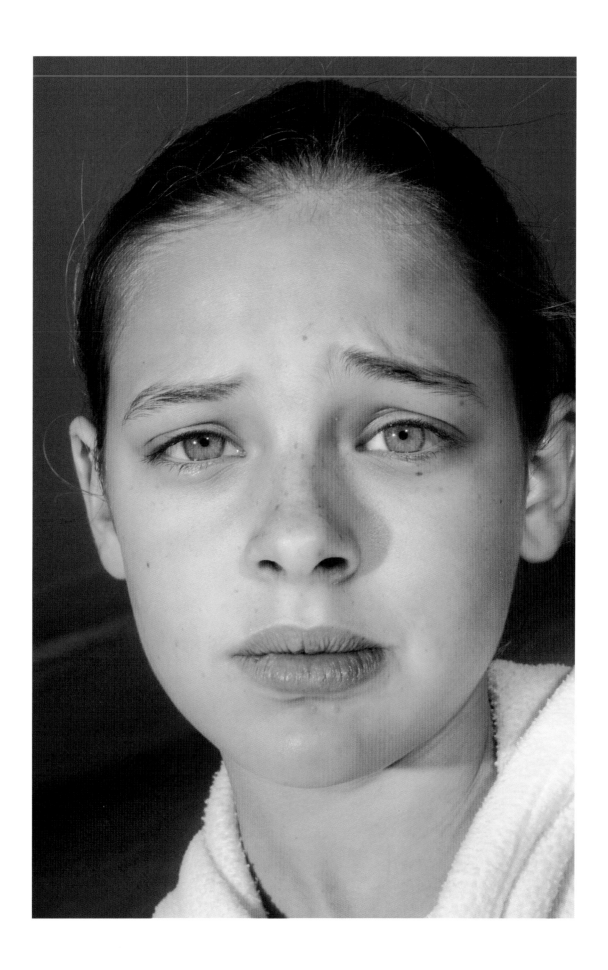

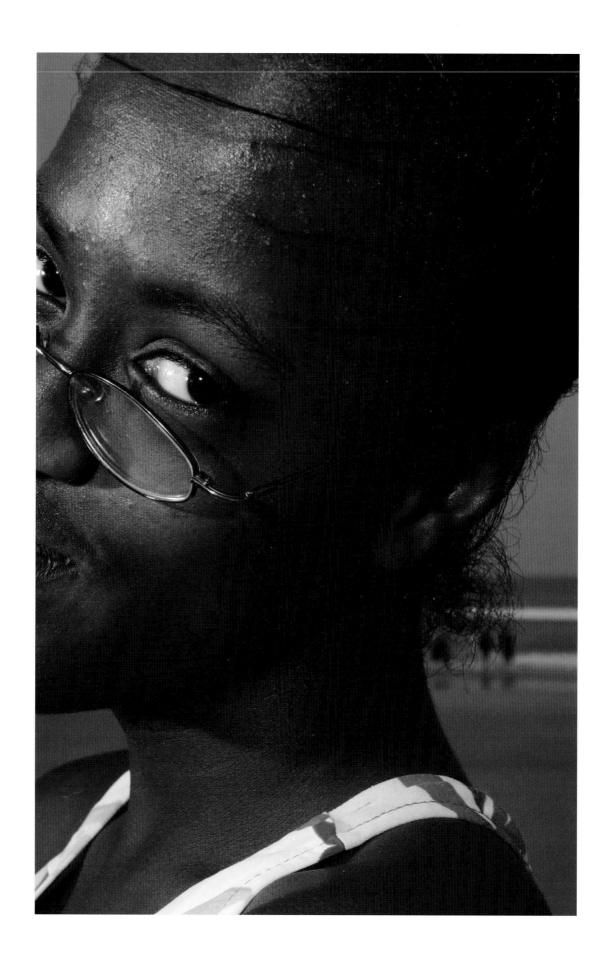

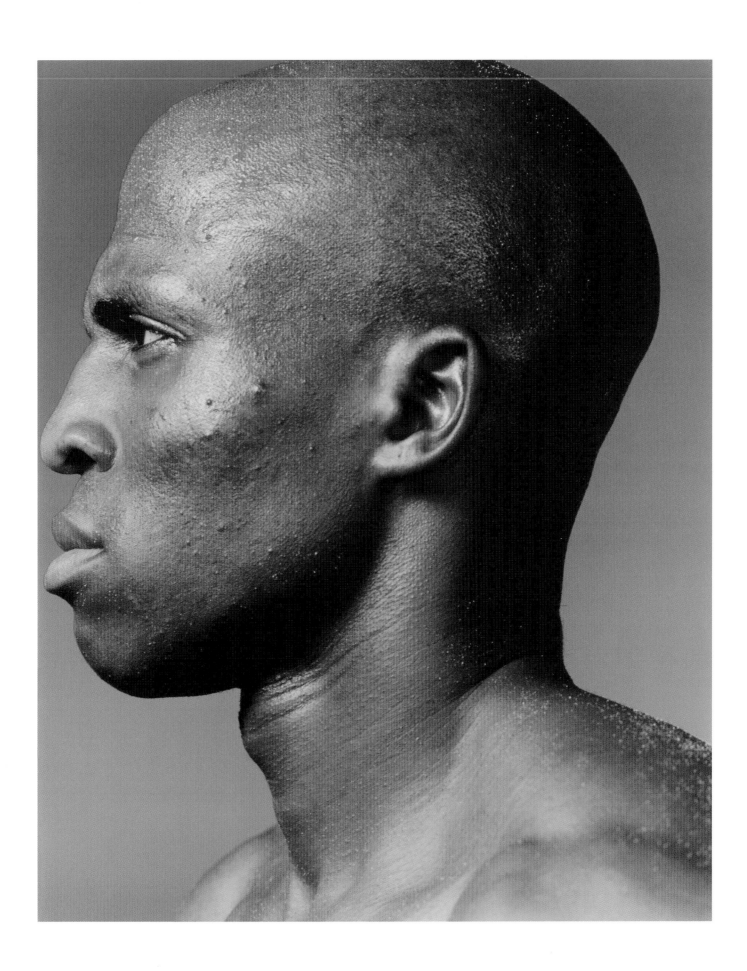